REDRAWING *the* MAP

The Formation and Dissolution of the Soviet Union

BUDD BAILEY

Cavendish Square

New York

Published in 2019 by Cavendish Square Publishing, LLC
243 5th Avenue, Suite 136, New York, NY 10016
Copyright © 2019 by Cavendish Square Publishing, LLC

First Edition

Cataloging-in-Publication Data
Names: Bailey, Budd.
Title: The formation and dissolution of the Soviet Union / Budd Bailey.
Description: New York : Cavendish Square, 2019. | Series: Redrawing the map | Includes glossary and index.
Identifiers: ISBN 9781502635679 (pbk.) | ISBN 9781502635655 (library bound) | ISBN 9781502635662 (ebook)
Subjects: LCSH: Russia (Federation)--Juvenile literature. | Russia (Federation)--History--Juvenile
literature. | Soviet Union--History--Juvenile literature. | Former Soviet republics--Juvenile literature.
Classification: LCC DK510.23 B35 2019 | DDC 947--dc23

Editorial Director: David McNamara
Editor: Erin L. McCoy
Copy Editor: Michele Suchomel-Casey
Associate Art Director: Amy Greenan
Designer: Jessica Nevins
Production Coordinator: Karol Szymczuk
Photo Research: J8 Media

Printed in the United States of America

CONTENTS

CHAPTER ONE

Mapmaking

I t takes only a quick look at a contemporary map of the Eastern Hemisphere to conclude that Russia is a powerful nation. Its territory encompasses part of eastern Europe, then sprawls all the way across northern Asia until it reaches the Pacific Ocean. Today, Russia is the largest nation on earth, twice as big as its runner-up in size, Canada.

Yet Russia used to be part of a country that was even bigger—in fact, it was one of the largest nations in the history of the planet, one whose history and politics would dramatically impact global events throughout the twentieth century.

A World Power

The Union of Soviet Socialist Republics—or as it's more commonly called, the Soviet Union or USSR—

RUSSIA

ARCTIC OCEAN

Wrangel Island

USA

BERING SEA

Svalbard

Zemlya Frantsa-Iosifa

Severnaya Zemlya

Novosibirskiye Ostrova

NORWAY

SWEDEN

FINLAND

Murmansk

Novaya Zemlya

Kamchatka Peninsula

Solovetsky Islands

Magadan

Vyborg

St Petersburg

0 ━━━━━ 1000 km
0 ━━━━━ 600 miles

BELARUS

Novgorod

Moscow

Sakhalin Island

Kursk

Perm

SIBERIA

Tynda

UKRAINE

Volga

Samara

Volgograd

Novosibirsk

Sochi

Irkutsk

Lake Baikal

GEORGIA

KAZAKHSTAN

Vladivostok

ARMENIA

MONGOLIA

CHINA

NORTH KOREA

CASPIAN SEA

UZBEKISTAN

IRAN

KYRGYZSTAN

Russia's borders are shown above as they are today, more than two decades after the fall of the Soviet Union. Former Soviet Socialist Republics, including Kazakhstan and Belarus, are now independent nations.

occupied the territory currently held by Russia and several of its neighbors. The USSR was formed in 1922 when the newly formed state absorbed other countries that shared its political and economic philosophy of Communism. Joining Russia to form this new country were Ukraine, Belarus, and the Transcaucasian Republic (which would later split into Armenia, Azerbaijan, and Georgia).

The territories of the Soviet Union increased during the next several years. For example, the Baltic states of Estonia, Latvia, and Lithuania were conquered around the start of World War II, thus ending about two decades of independence. Other countries that became part of the Soviet Union were Moldova, Kazakhstan, Kyrgyzstan, Tajikistan, Turkmenistan, and Uzbekistan.

The Soviet Union became one of history's most powerful empires. It competed with the United States for influence with other countries around the globe. Relations between the two nations were generally unfriendly, particularly beginning after World War II until the late 1980s. This period, and the geopolitical tensions that characterized it, became known as the Cold War.

Few thought the Soviet Union would disappear into the dust of history. However, that's exactly what happened when Soviet leader Mikhail Gorbachev signed a document on December 25, 1991, that brought an end to nearly seven decades of union.

THE LARGEST NATION ON EARTH

At its peak, the Soviet Union covered more than 8.6 million square miles (22.3 million square kilometers) of territory. That's more than twice as big as the United States. It extended in excess of 6,800 miles (10,943 km) from east to west and 2,800 miles (4,506 km) from north to south.

Head of state Mikhail Gorbachev signs a document on December 25, 1991, dissolving the Soviet Union.

The Geopolitics of Nationhood

The story of the Soviet Union is intertwined with geography. How could it not be? The nation shared a long border with China and was located only a few miles across the Bering Strait from Alaska. By the nineteenth century, ships from Russia could sail out of St. Petersburg and reach such nations as England, France, and Germany in just a week or so. Similar Soviet ships could leave from the USSR's southern ports, sail through the Black Sea and into the Mediterranean, and dock in southern Europe and northern Africa.

Yet for all of these potential points of contact with the rest of the world, the Soviet Union was insulated from many outside influences. Its leaders liked it that way. Trade between the USSR and Western nations was quite limited, making up only a small percentage of the Soviet economy. Most of its financial deals were with other Communist countries, which were often part of the Soviet empire, and with developing nations that had not taken sides in the Cold War.

To understand how geography defined the Soviet Union, we have to go back in time, before the USSR was founded. The history of Russia is complicated: its borders have been changing for more than a thousand years. One of the territory's earliest states, the Kievan Rus, disappeared shortly after its inception; other powerful nations surged up in its place and eventually grew into a vast, important country, like pieces of a jigsaw puzzle coming together. However, controlling such a large area isn't easy. Not only is it challenging to administer such a vast domain, Russia and the Soviet Union also had to prevent those living in smaller regions from seeking out their own independence— though many would eventually achieve it.

The story of Russia is also a story of its people, from its powerful and often brutal rulers, including Ivan the Terrible and Peter the Great, to a woman who had her own husband killed in order to take control of her country, to one of history's most murderous dictators. Then there are the modern-day leaders, such as Vladimir Putin. His actions show that efforts to redraw the Russian map aren't likely to cease any time soon.

It takes stepping back in history to understand how the Soviet Union came together, and how it fell apart.

CHAPTER TWO

Before the Creation of the Soviet Union

The origins of the Soviet Union go back more than eleven hundred years. The area between the Baltic Sea and the Black Sea back then was generally controlled by Slavic tribes. Each unit controlled a very small amount of territory, and influences on the region ranged all the way from Scandinavia to Iran.

Tribal Warfare and Power Clashes

Prince Oleg was the first ruler of the area to start collecting territory. Parts of the region banded together under Oleg's rule for trade and protection purposes in 882 CE; this federation came to be called the Kievan Rus. At the time, the region was called "land of the Rus," "Rus" being a term that referred to the people

Opposite: The Russian Revolution of 1917 set the stage for the formation of the Soviet Union.

there. Oleg placed the capital of the region in Kiev, located on the Dnieper River.

The Kievan Rus hoped to overpower another group in the area, the Khazars, who controlled the area between the Black Sea and the Caspian Sea, as well as considerable portions of land north of that region. The leaders of the Kievan Rus succeeded, adding territory through a war with the Khazars in the tenth century. By the middle of the eleventh century, the dominion of Kievan Rus was at its peak. It even had a written legal code used throughout the territory.

However, the glory of that confederation was about to decline. The Kievan Rus had a complicated relationship with the Byzantine Empire, a remnant of the Roman Empire, which had united much of Europe for centuries. The capital of the Byzantine Empire was Constantinople, which in the twelfth century was declining in strength. That caused a reduction in trade, which hurt the confederation's economy.

Then, the Mongol army arrived, led by legendary conqueror Genghis Khan. It had crossed most of Asia and wiped out practically everything in its path. The Kievan Rus saw an important victory in 1223, after which the Mongols retreated for more than a decade. However, in 1236, the Mongols returned with a vengeance. The invaders swept into the region again and rampaged through Kiev in 1240.

That was the end of the Kievan Rus. The area split into smaller, less powerful kingdoms that often engaged in small-scale wars amongst themselves. It stayed that way for about 250 years, during which time the roots of Russia, Belarus, and Ukraine began to take shape.

One of those kingdoms became known as the Grand Principality of Moscow, or, more simply, Muscovy. It was established in 1283 and was invaded an estimated 160 times over the next 250 years. Still, Muscovy became relatively prosperous in a short period of time, and during the fourteenth century, it started to stake a claim to the area formerly belonging to the Kievan Rus.

A game-changing event took place in 1462, when Ivan III—also known as Ivan the Great—took over as the leader of Muscovy. During his reign of more than forty years, Muscovy tripled in size. Under his leadership, the Golden Horde—the group of Mongols who had set up permanent residence in territories that would one day become Russia—was finally expelled from the region in 1480.

Ivan III's son, Vasily III, succeeded him and ruled for nearly thirty years. Then, after more than a decade of feuds for control, the state was passed on to Vasily III's son, Ivan IV, also called Ivan the Terrible. A better

REMAINS OF A GOLDEN HORDE CITY

In 2014, archaeologists announced that they had discovered the remains of Ukek, a city founded by the Golden Horde in the thirteenth century, along the Volga River. The city was multicultural, with residents practicing Shamanism, Islam, Christianity, and other religions.

Ivan the Terrible expanded the territorial holdings of Muscovy, playing a crucial role in creating what we now know as Russia.

translation of Ivan's nickname is Ivan the Formidable, so named because, until his death in 1584, Muscovy slowly but surely grew in size under the direction of this powerful and sometimes brutal ruler. No matter what you call him, he played a key role in shaping the eventual borders of Russia.

Both of Ivan's parents died by the time he was eight, and he was raised by members of the nobility. Ivan IV became the first person to take the title of tsar in 1547. His immediate goal was to take control of land along the Black Sea, which would be instrumental in the creation of trade routes connecting Muscovy with the rest of the world. By the end of the 1550s, Muscovy had expanded eastward to the Ural Mountains—something of an unofficial dividing line between Europe and Asia—and southward to the Caspian Sea.

In the quarter-century before his death in 1584, Ivan earned a reputation for instability and brutality. He took land away from citizens and gave it to his friends, created a secret police force, and showed signs of mental illness and paranoia. He beat his pregnant daughter-in-law and killed his son.

For the next few decades after Ivan's death, the Muscovite government went through a series of ineffective leaders from the Rurikid royal line. The unrest fomented by one of the most controversial of these leaders would lead to the rise of the Romanov dynasty, which would rule Russia for more than three hundred years. This leader, called the False Dmitry (the first of three so-named pretenders to the throne), took control in 1605. He alienated his supporters by appearing in public with Poles, whom he appeared to favor; he even dressed like one. Dmitry also sparked religious tensions in the country by attending a Roman Catholic church, outraging the Russian Orthodox majority. In 1606, he was assassinated and his body was burned. The ashes were loaded into a cannon and fired toward Poland. By 1613, the Romanovs were led by sixteen-year-old Michael, who claimed the title of tsar.

After overcoming conflicts with the Ottoman Empire, Muscovy turned its attention back to expansion. The global Age of Imperialism, in which several European nations sought to control territory in other parts of the world, would begin in earnest in the eighteenth century. However, years earlier, many great powers of the time had already committed to exploring the Western Hemisphere and the Far East and were now claiming as much territory as possible. Muscovy couldn't compete with these nations, in part because it didn't have a large navy. It could, however, expand to the east. Siberia, vast and almost empty except for a few tribes, spanned the entirety of northern Asia and was therefore ripe for the taking.

Muscovy's territory grew under Tsar Michael, who annexed land on the east side of the Urals. Explorers had reached the Pacific Ocean by 1638, and other parts of the region slowly came under Muscovy's control. By the 1650s, it had claimed most of Siberia. That meant

Muscovy stretched from eastern Europe all the way to the Pacific Ocean.

The possession of land is, in itself, no guarantee of success. Muscovy had traditionally been a somewhat closed society. The Russian Orthodox Church had a large say in the affairs of the country, and a general mistrust of foreigners and their ideas had taken hold, leading to general stagnation.

Yet, every so often, a person comes along who can change the course of a nation's history. Peter the Great was one of them.

The Rise of the Russian Empire

Peter I was born in 1672. He was involved in a struggle for power among family members from a young age. His older half brother, Tsar Fyodor III, died at the age of twenty in 1682, and his brother, Ivan V, had little interest in ascending the throne. Peter and Ivan split the responsibilities for a while, with Peter's mother keeping watch over him. Soon, however, an uprising resulted in the murder of several of Peter's relatives. Peter became embroiled in a final battle for power with his half sister, Sophia. After her supporters mounted an unsuccessful plot to claim the throne for her in 1698, Peter sent Sophia to a nunnery and had some of her backers killed. Peter had won, and Muscovy was given a new name as he was declared "Sovereign of All Russia" after Ivan's death in 1696.

Peter the Great, who ascended the throne in 1696, helped establish Russia's influence on a global scale.

A year later, Peter's ambitions for his country had become clear. He traveled to Amsterdam—then the world's richest city—as well as London and Vienna over a span of eighteen months. He got a firsthand look at how international trade helped the people of those nations. Upon returning in 1698, Peter went to work.

The Russian leader restructured the government, opened up trade, changed the alphabet, and started a newspaper. He added territory from Estonia, Latvia, and Finland—all nations along the Baltic Sea. Then, after a few conflicts with Turkey, Russia regained access to the Black Sea. Russia's ships were now free to travel throughout Europe.

Territorial acquisitions continued into the 1700s. Russia had seized land from Sweden in 1703, including the area where the Neva River and the Gulf of Finland met. That conflict was part of the Great Northern War, which stretched on for more than two decades and included an unsuccessful Swedish invasion attempt in 1709. The area at the mouth of the Neva was something of a swamp, but Peter ordered that a new city be built on the site. Peasants and prisoners of war did the work, and many of them died of malaria during the construction.

In 1712, St. Petersburg was born. Peter the Great moved the nation's capital from Moscow to his new city. London, Copenhagen, Amsterdam, Stockholm, and Oslo were only a short distance away by ship. St. Petersburg also was the ideal headquarters for the Russian navy, which Peter intended to expand. If there were ever trouble with Russia's neighbors, Peter would now be able to deploy these forces more quickly out of St. Petersburg.

Under the direction of Peter the Great, the city of St. Petersburg was founded in 1712 as a window to the West.

The Formation and Dissolution of the Soviet Union

There was a catch, however. St. Petersburg needed time to grow into a world-class city and port. Part of the problem was that ships needed to pass through a narrow channel at the eastern end of the Gulf of Finland, and the land surrounding that bay was controlled by Sweden. In the meantime, Russia's only maritime outlet in that part of the world was Arkangelsk, located northeast of St. Petersburg. However, that city's harbor, which opened into the White Sea, was frozen nine months out of the year.

A coalition of nations led by Russia finally wore down Sweden's forces. Sweden, which had been a regional power in the 1600s, sought peace in 1721, handing over four provinces near St. Petersburg to Russia. The new city's future was secured, and Russia quickly stepped into the power vacuum in the region caused by Sweden's loss of influence.

Peter—who would come to be known as Peter the Great—began to call his country's growing territory an empire and was declared emperor of Russia in 1721. The expansion continued when Peter sent his armies back to work in 1722 in a conflict with Persia, annexing the south and west coasts of the Caspian Sea for a short time.

In 1724, Peter jumped into the icy waters of the Gulf of Finland in an attempt to save a drowning soldier. Afterward, he grew ill. Peter died in 1725, leaving his country changed forever. No longer would Russia be a minor player in world events; it had become a major power.

Catherine the Great

Peter didn't pick a clear successor to lead the Russian Empire, and the title changed hands several times after his death. During that period of nearly forty years, Russia was involved in several international skirmishes, including a war with Turkey, and the empire gained some territory in Asia.

Finally, a powerful figure emerged who would once again redefine the Russian Empire and who would rule for more than three decades. Sophie Friederike Auguste was born a princess in Germany and in 1745 married Peter III, Peter the Great's grandson and nephew to Elizabeth, empress of Russia from 1741 to 1761. Sophie converted to the Russian Orthodox Church and gave herself a new name, Catherine.

After Elizabeth's death, Peter became emperor in January 1762. By that time, he was barely talking to his wife and preferred the company of other women. He

Catherine the Great expanded Russian territory to include parts of Poland and lands around the Black Sea.

made several unpopular decisions in the first months of his reign and even took land away from the powerful Russian Orthodox Church. After six months, Peter was overthrown and killed in a coup led by his own wife.

Catherine quickly made some important friends by bringing home troops who were engaged in a skirmish with Denmark and by returning land and property to the Orthodox Church. She then dove into foreign affairs. In 1772, Russia joined Prussia (the largest part of what was to become Germany) and Austria in splitting up Poland, a small nation too often caught in the middle of international conflicts. A peace treaty with the Ottoman Empire in 1774 secured new lands around the Black Sea, and Russia's influence in that region continued to grow with the annexation of the Crimean Peninsula in 1783.

Catherine died in 1796 and was succeeded by her son, Paul I, who reigned for five years until his assassination in 1801. His son, Alexander I, succeeded him and would soon face one of the greatest challenges to Russia's imperial expansion.

The Napoleonic Wars

While the Russian throne was changing hands in the 1790s, Napoleon Bonaparte was working his way up the ranks in the French military. He took power in 1799 and declared himself emperor of France in 1804. Napoleon then began his assault on other European nations. France's armies saw victory after victory as they swept through western and central Europe. They won out over Russian forces in Prussia in 1807, forcing Alexander to sign the secret Treaty of Tilsit.

That agreement joined Russia and France together as opponents of France's two major enemies, England and Sweden. Russian forces marched into Finland in 1808, annexing it into the Russian Empire. For the

An engraving shows defeated French soldiers returning to Paris after a failed attempt to invade Russia in 1812.

next century, Finland would retain many of its own laws and religious practices but take orders from Russia.

Napoleon had announced a sea blockade of Great Britain, but in 1810, Russia withdrew. Alexander thought the blockade was hurting the Russian economy. The move was not well received by France, and Napoleon immediately started raising a massive army.

On June 24, 1812, about five hundred thousand soldiers crossed into Russian territory. Troops came from all over Europe to join the force. "I have come once and for all to finish off these barbarians of the North," Napoleon purportedly said. At first, victory seemed imminent, as the Russians were forced to retreat while the French conquered city after city. However, they shocked Napoleon's forces by setting fire to abandoned areas as they left. This scorched-earth policy ensured that nothing left behind could be used by the French. With supply lines stretched beyond their limit, French soldiers soon ran out of food and ammunition.

The French army marched into Moscow in September, only to find much of the city in flames and its food supply gone. With temperatures dropping and winter fast approaching, Napoleon and his army fled the city. The retreat was difficult, as there was no source of food along the way. Meanwhile, the Russian army attacked repeatedly from the sides and the rear. Napoleon avoided complete disaster when his troops reached the border, but by then, most of his forces had been killed or wounded. Russia had successfully defended its territory. The French leader tried to regroup, but his position in Europe continued to deteriorate until Paris fell in 1814.

New Challenges

Russia sensed a new opportunity to expand its territory and influence in the middle of the nineteenth century. The Ottoman Empire had declined by that time, leaving a power vacuum that the Russians hoped to fill. But England and France partnered with the Ottoman Turks to take a stand against Russia in the Crimean War (1853–1856). The Russians lost about two hundred thousand troops on the battlefield against the small but modernized forces of their opponents, and they were in danger of the British invading St. Petersburg when a peace treaty was finally signed. It was a devastating defeat for the Russians, who were no match for their opponents in terms of weapons and technology.

Russia was close to broke after that war and needed funds badly. The nation decided to sell its North American territory known as Alaska to the United States. Even so, Russia continued to pursue expansionist policies to the southwest, picking up some territory along the way.

At the same time, the Russian leadership hadn't forgotten the Far East. It had an interest in extending its reach in that part of the world, mostly in the regions of Manchuria (now part of China) and Korea, early in the twentieth century. This brought it into conflict with Japan. When Russia backed out of an agreement to withdraw, Japan attacked in 1904. It was a quick war, lasting about a year, as Russia couldn't match Japan's forces or its geographical advantage. US president Theodore Roosevelt helped negotiate a peace treaty.

The conflict was never popular in Russia, and the loss—the first by a European nation to an Asian counterpart—deepened that dissatisfaction. It led to a 1905 attempt at revolution led by Vladimir Lenin and

During the first half of the eighteenth century, Russia owned a massive territory in the Western Hemisphere: Alaska. It was right across the Bering Strait from Russian territory, and the Russian-American Company was earning large profits on products from that land.

Even so, Alaska was a long, long way from St. Petersburg, the capital of Russia, so when the Crimean War broke out in the 1850s, Russia realized that it could not effectively defend its North American territory. What's more, Russia lost that war and suffered financial problems as a result. It began talks with the United States in the 1860s over the possible sale of Alaska. The process was slowed by the American Civil War, but the two sides completed the deal in 1867. The price was a mere $7.2 million ($113.8 million in today's dollars), which came out as two cents per acre.

The transaction was negotiated by William Seward. Seward had been governor of New York and wanted to be president of the United States. However, he lost the Republican nomination to Abraham Lincoln in 1860 and instead became Lincoln's secretary of state. He stayed on the job after Lincoln's assassination in 1865.

People on both sides were unhappy about the sale. Russia had invested money and effort into Alaska and thought its financial return was too low. Americans wondered what they could gain from this chilly region, located so far away from other US territory. The deal was known as "Seward's Folly" for some time afterward.

The United States did little with its new Alaskan lands after the purchase was completed. The federal government more or less ignored it for seventeen years and didn't put a civil government in place until 1884. But the transaction proved worthwhile for the Americans in the long run. Opinions about Alaska changed when the Klondike gold rush in the 1890s brought in hundreds of millions in dollars. Oil fields in northern Alaska later added value to America's investment. The deal also helped the United States increase its commercial ties to Asian nations.

the Bolsheviks, later called the Russian Communist Party. In the aftermath of the uprising, Tsar Nicholas II gave up some of his power but managed to retain his position as leader of the Russian Empire. Troops from the Russo-Japanese War were used to restore order in late 1905.

However, Nicholas's problems were far from over. World War I was just the push the nation needed to fall into chaos, and by the beginning of 1917, Russia was ripe for massive change.

A Communist Nation

The war did not start off well for Russia, which was fighting on the side of England and France. Its leadership was not well equipped to lead the nation into such a huge conflict. The country's economic situation slowly grew more desperate, and food shortages were widespread. When riots broke out in March 1917, soldiers were unwilling to stop their fellow Russians from protesting.

In just a few days, Tsar Nicholas II was overthrown from his position. His brother, Grand Duke Michael, turned down the chance to succeed him, and the Romanov family dynasty that had ruled Russia for more than three hundred years came to an end.

A temporary government was set up to oversee Russia while order was restored. Its leadership consisted of some of the nation's elites: bankers, lawyers, and businessmen. However, those leaders prolonged Russia's

Vladimir Lenin is shown giving a speech to Vsevobuch servicemen on May 25, 1919, one year after the Soviet armed forces were founded.

involvement in World War I, despite having promised to withdraw. Bolshevik leader Lenin—back in Russia after a period in exile—set up a rival group called the Petrograd Soviet of Workers' and Soldiers' Deputies. Its membership consisted of factory workers and soldiers, representing the nonelite classes and placing it in stark contrast with the Provisional Government leadership.

The government reorganized four times in the summer of 1917, but the nation continued to spiral deeper into chaos. Finally, the Bolsheviks staged a revolution that toppled the Provisional Government and took control of Russia, an uprising called the October Revolution.

Civil War

The transition would prove difficult, however. Several groups opposed the Communists, and some of them wanted the tsar returned to power. The Russian Civil War broke out between the Bolsheviks—nicknamed the Reds—and the opposing groups, known as the Whites. Lenin's first step as head of government was to extract the country from World War I as quickly as possible.

When Russia surrendered to Germany and Austria-Hungary in the Treaties of Brest-Litovsk in 1918, several regions of western and southwestern Russia became independent nations. More than sixty million people in Estonia, Latvia, Lithuania, Belarus, and Ukraine no longer pledged allegiance to the Russian flag. The Germans sent soldiers into these areas as an occupying force—troops that might have been instrumental in western Europe later that year. Soon, Germany collapsed, and the Allies (United States, Britain, and France) won World War I. Russia then declared the Treaties of Brest-Litovsk void, and Bolshevik groups went to work. Their goal was to consolidate control in Russia, but they had to win the civil war first.

The Whites were never completely unified during the civil war, so the Bolsheviks took them on one at a time and defeated them. By 1921, Lenin and the Bolsheviks had emerged victorious: they were in control of the entire nation. Russia, however, was in terrible shape. All of its major industries, including agriculture, had collapsed, and at least five million people had died. Law and order had broken down.

Building a Union

Meanwhile, some of the nations bordering Russia during that period were in no better condition than their massive neighbor. Lenin would have preferred for other countries to realize that Communism was inevitable and to then freely join Russia in achieving that goal. "We want a voluntary union of nations—a union which precludes any coercion of one nation by another—a union founded on complete confidence, on a clear recognition of brotherly unity, on absolutely voluntary consent," Lenin declared—a quote that now appears on the wall of the Central Lenin Museum.

In reality, unity was achieved out of the barrel of a gun. One of those border nations was Ukraine, which in late 1917 had become embroiled in a war with the Bolsheviks, who were attempting to expand Russian territory. Ukrainian forces fought off the Russians until the Treaties of Brest-Litovsk were signed. Ukraine then

Opposite: A world atlas from 1923 shows the newly formed Soviet Union in yellow. Such regions as Ukraine and Belarus (today independent nations) are shown as part of the USSR in this map.

became an independent nation until the end of World War I, when Russian forces invaded. The conflict between the two nations lasted until 1921, when the Bolsheviks won a decisive battle and Ukraine was divided among four states, one of which was called the Ukrainian Socialist Soviet Republic and remained under Bolshevik control; it was incorporated into the USSR in 1922.

It was easier for the Russians to take control of Belarus and other nearby territories. Once the Germans had lost World War I, the Russians marched in and conquered the country. It took less than two months for the Belorussian Soviet Socialist Republic to be formed. Azerbaijan, on the Caspian Sea to the south, had enjoyed its independent status for about two years (1918–1920) before Bolshevik troops arrived, and soon the republic was captured and renamed the Soviet Socialist Republic of Azerbaijan. In 1922, Azerbaijan and its neighbors, Georgia and Armenia, were formally annexed by the Soviets and formed the Transcaucasian Soviet Federated Socialist Republic.

A formal arrangement was needed for the political entities to come together, and the nations signed a treaty to do just that in 1922. This treaty created the Union of Soviet Socialist Republics. The new joint government was something of a compromise. One idea had been to have Russia swallow up the other nations under its control, while others preferred to form a loose federation of those republics. The adopted plan fell in between these two options.

The ruling government quickly set up a centralized political system. The constituent republics' rights to governance were restricted to domestic and cultural affairs, while all political issues and many other government functions were controlled by those in power in Moscow, which had replaced St. Petersburg as the country's capital in 1918. Non-Communist political parties in the constituent republics lost their right to participate in government, and some of their leaders were exiled to other nations.

The creation of a new nation based on socialist principles—in which the governing party would in theory represent the class of wage earners and economic production would be closely controlled by the state—hadn't been easy. The Soviet Union was disorganized and weak at its birth in 1922, but its size gave it a chance to become mighty.

CHAPTER THREE

The Geography of the USSR

The USSR was the largest country on earth. It was more than two and a half times as big as the United States. If you somehow took the country and wrapped it around the planet Pluto, it would cover it up completely. The USSR bordered on both Finland and North Korea—countries that are more than 4,000 miles (6,437 km) apart. The Soviet Union was only 2.5 miles (4 km) away from the United States at one point on the map, this being the distance between a pair of islands in the Bering Sea.

Perhaps the most telling way to measure the USSR's size is by how many time zones it crossed. There are twenty-four time zones around the world, each of them about 1,000 miles (1,609 km) across at the equator. The Soviet Union had eleven time zones—almost half of the entire globe's total.

Between 1917 and 1922, a number of territories were incorporated into the USSR, including Ukraine and Belarus (*shown partly in yellow*).

The country's new government finally caught up with much of the rest of the world in 1919 by adopting time zones. Before that, every city in Russia had its own time, based on the sun, so every time a citizen traveled more than a handful of miles east or west, he or she had to find out what time it was in the new location. To add to the confusion, all railroads in the country used St. Petersburg's time for their timetables. You could be in Vladivostok on the Sea of Japan near the Korean peninsula, and the trains still ran according to what time it was 4,000 miles (6,437 km) to the west.

The Pros and Cons of a Massive Nation

The Soviet Union's size was its ticket to becoming a world power. Its vast territories ensured access to a great many natural resources, including deposits of minerals valued throughout the world.

For example, we often think of the Middle East as the biggest oil-producing region in the world, but in fact, the Soviet Union at its height had control of more oil than any other nation on earth. The same was true for natural gas, and the USSR was third worldwide in coal reserves.

However, there are drawbacks to owning so much land. The USSR had to defend a great deal of territory. It shared thousands of miles of borders with other countries. The military was spread out over a huge area, so it was expensive and logistically challenging to maintain. In fact, this last problem may have contributed to the demise of the USSR.

Russia had already encountered these challenges. The circumstances surrounding the Russo-Japanese War were a prime example of the disadvantages of defending such a big country. When the Japanese attacked Russia in 1904 over a dispute on the Asian mainland, the Russian fleet had to travel thousands of miles—all the way from the Baltic Sea—in order to defend national

Wagons filled with petroleum are pictured in petrochemical center Nizhnekamsk, Russia, in 2015. Natural resources such as oil provided the Soviet Union with several economic advantages.

interests. What's more, conflicts such as this one, thousands of miles away from the country's capital, were not backed by much popular support. Most of the Russian population was located in Europe, and few had any interest in defending territory in the Far East.

Meanwhile, much of the USSR's coastline bordered the Arctic Ocean. It was far enough north that the water was frozen for several months out of the year, so the area was of little use for shipping and other commercial purposes. Then, when the spring thaw finally arrived in northern Russia, it often brought flooding with it. The Soviet Union's Pacific coast was almost as cold, with mountain ranges cutting off the area from the rest of the mainland and limiting the economic impact of seaports.

Building viable infrastructure across eleven time zones was also a challenge, particularly since a significant portion of the USSR was either near or above the Arctic Circle, where the average temperature rarely gets above 50 degrees Fahrenheit (10 degrees Celsius). Roads were difficult to build. Railroads had to deal with cold temperatures and snow that might stay on the ground for months. Stringing telephone and telegraph lines across those vast distances—and then maintaining them—was a major project.

The Russians did build the Trans-Siberian Railroad early in the twentieth century, which helped bring the nation together during its time as the Soviet Union. The train line, which stretches 5,772 miles (9,289 km) from Moscow to Vladivostok, continues to operate—and is still being expanded—to this day. It takes more than six days to travel from one end of the line to the other.

The Trans-Siberian Railroad could be compared to the United States' transcontinental railroad, which was built in the 1860s and 1870s. However, once America's new railroad route was built, parts of the western United States were ripe for settlement and development; new railroads were created almost overnight, and the western half of the United States grew quickly. In comparison, economic development in the isolated portions of Russia and the Soviet Union— with its rugged climate and challenging terrain—didn't come as easily.

Construction of the Trans-Siberian Railroad was difficult and costly, but it brought the vast nation of Russia closer together.

Water Access and Fertile Land

The Soviet Union was generally considered a European country because most of its people lived on that continent. However, a majority of the USSR's land was in Asia. The natural dividing line between the two continents is the Ural mountain range, which runs from north to south, starting in the Arctic Circle. The Urals are the oldest mountains in the world and have been worn down by erosion over the years. That's why the tallest mountain in the range, Mount Narodnaya, checks in at only 6,217 feet (1,894 meters) tall.

Western Russia's higher population may, in large part, be attributable to its ample access to water. At the

DIVERSITY IN THE USSR

The Soviet Union was an incredibly diverse nation. In 1929, it had 182 different ethnic groups that spoke 149 different languages.

height of the Soviet Union's range, there were about 150,000 rivers of at least 6 miles (9.6 km) in length, and most of them were navigable. Several large rivers ran through the western USSR, and much of the population lived along or near those rivers. The Volga stretches more than 2,200 miles (3,540 km) before reaching the Caspian Sea, while the Dnieper River flows past Kiev in the region of Ukraine and continues south into the Black Sea.

The region of the Soviet Union just north of the Black Sea had—and still has—the most moderate climate in the country. Sochi, the site of the 2014 Winter Olympics, is located on the shoreline in that region, and even in January, the average low temperature is above freezing. That made it very attractive to the Soviet government, whose leaders wasted little time in taking advantage of its warmer weather. They built health resorts on the shore of the Black Sea soon after the Russian Revolution of 1917.

The area was also strategically important as the nation sought to extend its influence. It was a short trip from the Black Sea to the Mediterranean Sea, so Soviet military vessels were never too far from southern Europe and North Africa.

The Volga River, pictured here near Samara in west-central Russia, is one of the longest and most important waterways in the country.

The western USSR also had more access to fertile land. The European Plain begins at the border between France and Spain and crosses western and northern France, through Belgium and the Netherlands, moving on through Germany, Poland, and eastern Europe, finally stretching across Russian territory until it bumps into the Ural Mountains. Because several large rivers pass through the region, it's relatively easy to divert the waters for irrigation, which in turn has ensured its agricultural success. Farms in this plain are plentiful and productive, and for this reason, it's been called the breadbasket of Europe.

When the Soviet Union was founded in 1922, it had a key natural advantage. Ukraine, which joined with Russia and other republics to form the USSR, was one of the most fertile agricultural areas in the world and had produced essential food crops such as wheat for generations.

However, Soviet leadership gave up this natural advantage for political reasons. The Communist Party's political support came primarily from industrial workers. Ukraine's farmers had at first joined these workers in welcoming the new economic system, but the peasants believed that they would be able to own land after the Russian Revolution, and that assumption proved very wrong. Land and inventory were confiscated and redistributed, angering especially the richer peasants, or kulaks, whom the government styled as class enemies of the poor. In 1929, Joseph Stalin initiated systematic attacks on the kulaks: an estimated 10 million—1.2 million of whom were from Ukraine—were exiled to Siberia. It is estimated that about half of those Ukrainians died in exile. Meanwhile, the expulsion of so many farmers left much of the region's arable land without skilled laborers, resulting in a famine that lasted for years.

Farming is still a large part of Ukraine's economy today. It employs about one-quarter of the nation's working population.

However, once the plain meets the Ural Mountains, the climate changes. Storms rolling in from the west hit the mountains and deposit precipitation there, leaving Siberia, on the east side of the range, relatively dry. Much of the ground in central Siberia remains permanently frozen, and while summers can be dusty and dry, winter temperatures are the lowest on earth outside of Antarctica.

While the European regions of the Soviet Union had ample access to water, much of the country's Asian regions were not so lucky. Deserts are common in central Asia. Vegetation sometimes burns away during the summer months, and irrigation is both difficult and expensive.

Resource Access and Conflict

Good agricultural land is highly desirable, and any nation that controls such territories ensures that it doesn't need to rely on imports to feed its population. Such independence was a priority for the USSR, given that only 10 percent of its land was considered arable—that is, suitable for growing crops. Much of its land was too far north to sustain agriculture.

What's more, Russia had trailed behind the rest of Europe when it came to industrialization and modernization. Over the years, that made it a tempting target for invaders, who often believed that it would be easy to conquer. There are no natural obstacles to deter European armies. As a result, Russia had been forced to defend itself on a regular basis: from Poland in 1605, Sweden in 1707, France in 1812, and Germany in 1914. Given this long history of assault by foreign invaders, a sharp awareness of the country's geographical insecurity has played a key role in how Russia and the Soviet Union have defined their role in the world.

The USSR's most famous leader, Joseph Stalin, was keenly aware of this threat and sought to violently suppress any challenges to the country's hegemony (that is, its influence or authority), both inside and outside its borders. Stalin would come to be known as one of the most ruthless dictators in the world. When political rivals did not agree with him, they were frequently jailed or killed. The same fate awaited those farmers who opposed the abolishment of private land ownership in favor of grouping their farms into larger, single units—a process called collectivization, implemented to boost food production and support the Soviet Union's efforts to become a world power.

The 1930s saw the rise of German chancellor Adolf Hitler and the German war machine. The Soviets thought they had solved the problem by signing a nonaggression treaty with Germany in 1939, so when the Germans invaded Poland from the west in 1939, the Soviets did the same from the east and occupied more than half of that nation. In 1940, the Soviet Union formally swallowed up the small Baltic states of Estonia, Latvia, and Lithuania, making them the newest members of the Soviet Union.

Joseph Stalin led the Soviet Union for almost thirty years.

However, the Soviets had to change their allegiances in 1941. Thanks to his alliance with the USSR, Hitler had bought time for his war machine to conquer much of western Europe. Now he turned his sights to the east and launched an attack on the Soviet Union. Hitler had a powerful fighting force, numbering three million soldiers on the eastern front alone. Germany was counting on a quick victory, but after some initial successes, the harsh Soviet winter again took its toll. The Germans were forced to retreat. By 1944, Germany faced large armed forces to its east and west. Both sides slowly worked their way toward a meeting point in Berlin. The Allies (the United States, England, France, and the USSR) emerged victorious in 1945.

Europe, which had been devastated by more than five years of conflict, was essentially split into two parts after World War II ended. The line went right through the middle of Germany, splitting it into two separate nations. The Soviets were granted the right to occupy and oversee territory in eastern Europe. They couldn't officially annex such nations as Poland, Czechoslovakia, Hungary, Romania, and Bulgaria into the USSR, but they could control them by installing puppet governments. This approach significantly expanded the amount of territory under Soviet influence and kept the armies of the other Allies farther from Soviet borders.

After the end of World War II, the capitalist United States and the Communist Soviet Union grew increasingly at odds with one another, each working under the assumption that the other wanted to dominate the world and disseminate its own political system. This mounting tension came to be known as the Cold War.

A map of the Eastern Hemisphere helps to explain the value that both sides of the Cold War placed on Eastern Europe. It was the bridge between Europe and Asia, and both capitalist and Communist nations wanted to control that key strategic region.

NAMING THE COLD WAR

The phrase "Cold War" was first used by George Orwell in 1945. He was the author of *Animal Farm*, which satirized Stalin's rule over the Soviet Union.

While Eastern Europe technically wasn't part of the USSR, it was certainly part of the Soviet sphere of influence. By the 1950s, the USSR was 8.65 million square miles (22.4 million sq km) in size, but it would have totaled more than 14 million square miles (36.3 million sq km) if other Communist countries had been included. The country's immense size made it seem as though the Soviet Union would be around for centuries.

Instead, it was gone by 1992.

CHAPTER FOUR
The Cold War and the Fall of the USSR

By 1979, the Soviet Union had been one of the world's most powerful nations for decades, having emerged as a superpower after the end of World War II. The Soviets had gained control of several Eastern European nations shortly after the war, and their influence in the region remained formidable.

Any resistance to Soviet hegemony in the region had been swiftly repressed. Polish protestors had won some concessions from the government early in 1956, and Hungary tried to do the same later that year. After some indecision in Moscow, leaders there sent Soviet troops into Hungary to crush the rebellion. More than 2,500 Hungarians were killed. Czechoslovakian protestors met the same fate in 1968, when 137 people were killed. It seemed that the status quo would last indefinitely.

Opposite: The fall of the Berlin Wall in 1989 was a major event in the USSR's decline.

However, as powerful as the USSR seemed, the road toward its eventual dissolution began in 1979.

A Clash of Political Ideologies

By 1979, the United States and its allies, including Great Britain and France, had been pursuing a policy of containment when it came to the Soviet Union for more than thirty years. The goal was to give up no more territory to Communist countries. The policy had been developed by longtime US government official George Kennan, who wrote a column in 1947 for the journal *Foreign Affairs.* "The main element of any United States policy toward the Soviet Union must be that of a long-term, patient but firm and vigilant containment of Russian expansive tendencies," Kennan wrote.

There was some debate among government officials on the effectiveness of the strategy. Some thought that it was too defensive and that the United States' ultimate goal should be to roll back the Soviet Union's gains in every part of the world. But Kennan's view ultimately won out, and his approach defined the foreign policy of the United States for the next forty-plus years.

This policy of containment was adopted too late to change the course of history in China, which was in the midst of a civil war between the Nationalist Party and the Chinese Communist Party (CCP). The Communists took control of the country in 1949, and later that year, China and the Soviet Union agreed to a treaty of friendship. The relationship between those two countries had its ups and downs over the years, but China remains under the control of the CCP to this day.

Also in 1949, the United States joined with Canada and several Western European nations to form the North Atlantic Treaty Organization (NATO). It served as a united front against Communist aggression in Europe. The containment policy twice led to major military action by the Americans—in the Korean War in the early 1950s and in the Vietnam War (1954–1975). Overall, the policy met with limited success: Communist North Korea held onto its territory after three years of war, and South Vietnam fell to forces from Communist North Vietnam in 1975.

Growing Unrest

However, the demise of the Soviet Union began not during these conflicts, but later, in the central Asian nation of Afghanistan. Paired with the growing unrest in Poland in 1979 and a tense relationship with the United States, this conflict heralded the beginning of the end of the Soviet Union.

Conflict in Afghanistan

Afghanistan is a large country bordered by Pakistan and Iran, and it was once something of a gateway between Europe and Asia. In its early history, it was invaded and conquered by such famous leaders as Alexander the Great and Genghis Khan. Afghanistan wasn't united as a single nation until the eighteenth century. Great Britain fought three wars with Afghanistan between 1838 and 1921, in part to protect its interests in nearby India.

Afghanistan is very mountainous, making any sort of travel difficult. The exception is in the south and west, where the land is mostly desert. As a result of these geographical obstacles, communication throughout the country has been extremely difficult, making the nation difficult to govern from a central authority. Instead, the people of Afghanistan have remained loyal to their regional tribes and to their religious principles. Many Afghans have often proved very conservative in terms of social change.

The country enjoyed a few decades of relative peace from the 1930s until the 1970s. Kabul, the capital city, was considered a very beautiful place. However, Afghanistan's recent history has been less than tranquil. Zahir Shah became king in 1933 and ruled until he was deposed in 1973. His cousin, General Mohammed Daud Khan, who had been prime minister from 1953 to 1963, named himself president after the political uprising. He served in that office for only five years, until he was assassinated in another coup in 1978.

Nur Mohammad Taraki, one of the founding members of the People's Democratic Party of Afghanistan—a Communist organization—became the new president. The new leader said he would end the country's close relationship with the Soviet Union and stick to Islamic principles in ruling the nation. At

Soviet armored vehicles arrive in Kabul on January 30, 1980. The Soviet Union's invasion of Afghanistan proved to be a blunder.

the same time, conservative forces in rural areas still objected to reforms that had been introduced by Daud Khan. Afghanistan had been torn into several factions by 1979, when Taraki was killed by supporters of Hafizullah Amin, the deputy prime minister.

Afghanistan was in turmoil when, on December 24, 1979, the Soviet Union took the unprecedented step of invading its neighbor. Amin was executed three days later. The Soviets thought they could restore a strong relationship with the Afghan government and increase their influence in southern Asia by putting someone new (in this case, Deputy Prime Minister Babrak Karmal) in charge.

However, with a pro-Soviet government in place and the USSR's military forces occupying the nation, a new set of problems emerged. The invasion united all of the other groups into one opposition faction. The Soviet Union was about to discover the same lesson that past invading forces had learned again and again: it was easy to get into Afghanistan, but difficult to get out.

Poland and the Pope

The year 1979 also saw the beginnings of unrest in Poland, starting with a series of speeches by a religious figure. Karol Wojtyla, who had been the archbishop of Krakow, Poland, had been elected pope in 1978. He took the name Pope John Paul II. Yuri Andropov, then head of the Soviet Union's domestic security and foreign intelligence agency, called the KGB, and a future leader of the USSR, ordered a study into how Wojtyla's ascendancy to one of the world's most influential religious offices would affect world events. The study concluded that it would destabilize Poland and make it more difficult for the Soviets to maintain absolute control over Eastern European satellite nations.

On June 5, 1979, the pope kissed the ground when he arrived in Warsaw, Poland, on an official visit. He

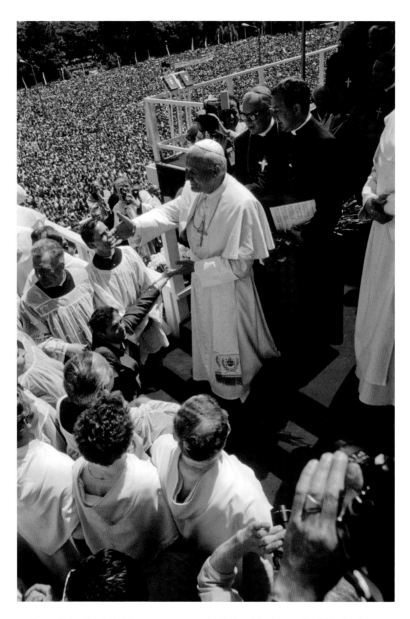

Pope John Paul II visits a monastery in Poland in June of 1979. During this visit, he spoke out against the USSR's policy of state atheism.

reminded the Poles of their religious heritage, an act that was strongly discouraged by the USSR's state atheism doctrine. "You are not who they say you are, so let me remind you who you are," the pope told the people of his home country. On the same trip, he also told the Poles that history was a tool in day-to-day life. "Fidelity to roots does not mean a mechanical copying of the patterns of the past," he said. "Fidelity to roots is always creative, ready to descend into the depths, open to new challenges." Considering that the official Soviet government policy was to suppress rather than celebrate the past, such speeches had an electric effect on the Polish people.

A few months later, the Communist Party of the Soviet Union sent out this order to the KGB: "Use all possibilities available to the Soviet Union to prevent the new course of policies initiated by the Polish pope; if necessary with additional measures beyond disinformation and discreditation."

The first cracks in the Communists' control of the satellite nations appeared in an unlikely place—the shipyards of Gdansk, Poland. Workers there had banded together in 1970 to protest working conditions; the efforts had been quickly squashed by Polish authorities. The leaders of this new trade union—which went by the name of Solidarity—had been worried that the strike would not attract enough attention across Poland to force the government to negotiate. But this time was different. The 1980 strike caught the world's attention. How would the Polish government respond to this situation?

The surprising answer came at the end of August 1980. The Polish government signed three separate agreements allowing the unions to exist, giving them the right to strike and offering more political and religious freedom. It was an unprecedented moment. Within a year, a labor union had been formally created, and a large part of the workforce of Poland—ten million strong—had joined.

During 1981, another development rocked the situation in Western Europe. On May 13, a Turkish assassin named Mehmet Ali Agca fired four shots at Pope John Paul II. The bullets did not hit any vital organs, and the pontiff recovered from surgery over the next few weeks. The motives of the assassin remain murky, but some believe he was carrying out the orders of the Soviet government through the Bulgarian secret police.

Back in Poland, few thought that the Soviets would stand for such a strong opposition force to exist indefinitely. In late 1981, martial law was declared within the Polish borders. Solidarity was, for all practical purposes, shut down, and life in that country returned to what it had been for the last several decades. Still, ideas of change had been planted in the minds of many Poles, and it would remain there.

Tensions with the United States

Meanwhile, the relationship between the United States and the Soviet Union was poised to change after the American election of 1980. Challenger Ronald Reagan, a hard-line voice against Communism, had defeated President Jimmy Carter and would soon alter the course of American foreign policy.

Leonid Brezhnev died in 1982, ending an eighteen-year career as the leader of the Soviet Union. While he had been friendly to the West in some respects, he had maintained strict control over fellow Communist countries in the Eastern Bloc. Yuri Andropov took over for Brezhnev as general secretary of the Communist Party. He tried to revive the weak Soviet economy and made few attempts to warm relations with the West.

President Reagan responded early in 1983 with a proposal to begin work on a Strategic Defense Initiative that became known as the Star Wars program. The goal was to develop technology capable of shooting down Soviet-launched missiles before they reached United States territory. Both nations had been developing and stockpiling nuclear arms and long-range weapons for years, which had contributed to mounting Cold War tensions. The Star Wars defensive system was an expensive proposition that would require a great many steps forward in research and technology before it could actually be used. It was a major escalation in the arms race between the two countries, and the Soviets knew they didn't have the financial resources to keep up.

The United States' plans to build a missile defense program led to protests around the world, including in the United Kingdom.

Later in 1983, the Soviets shot down a South Korean airliner that had accidentally crossed into their airspace on the way to Seoul, purportedly mistaking the aircraft for a US spy plane. A total of 269 civilians died in the incident, which the Soviets at first denied had even happened. Later, USSR officials acknowledged the attack, but did not apologize and blamed the US Central Intelligence Agency (CIA). From there, the Soviet Union broke off missile reduction talks with the United States, turning the Cold War even colder.

Andropov hadn't been in good health since early in 1983, and he died in the spring of 1984. Konstantin Chernenko became the next general secretary of the USSR. He had been a candidate to replace Brezhnev in 1982 and now opted to return to Brezhnev's hard-line approach to relations with the West. Chernenko ordered the Soviet Union's boycott of the 1984 Summer Olympics in Los Angeles, a response to an American boycott of the 1980 Games in Moscow, which had in turn been a protest against the Soviet occupation of Afghanistan.

However, the new general secretary, now in his early seventies, suffered health problems for almost his entire tenure. On March 10, 1985, funeral music again played on official state radio channels in the USSR—this time for Chernenko. For the third time in as many years, the search began for another leader of the Soviet Union.

This time, that search led to the promotion of a very different type of leader.

Mikhail Gorbachev, who became the Soviet head of state in 1985, is pictured during a visit to London in April 1989.

A Collapsing Nation

Mikhail Gorbachev was the son of peasants. His grandfather, Pantelei Gopkalo, was arrested and tortured in prison for fourteen months during Joseph Stalin's Great Purge of the 1930s. His father, Sergei, fought for the Soviets in World War II and was wounded. Sergei returned home to southern Russia and resumed his career working with farm machinery. Mikhail was a good student, and after high school, he was accepted into Moscow University, the USSR's top college. He graduated with a law degree in 1955.

From there he started to work his way up the ladder of the Communist Party, earning a reputation for dedication and organization. By 1980, Gorbachev was the head of the Politburo, the executive committee that ran the Soviet government. He was considered a contender for the nation's top position after the deaths of Brezhnev and Andropov but was not selected. However, when yet another election took place in 1985, he was ready and won.

Gorbachev took over a nation that was in deep trouble. The economy was slowing, health care was disintegrating, and the mortality rate was rising. Meanwhile, the Soviets' costly adventure into Afghanistan was showing no signs of ending. What's more, governing such a vast empire, including the satellite states in Eastern Europe, was proving to be expensive. Geography was working against the Soviets, and a mighty military could not change the situation.

When it came to addressing these problems, Gorbachev had few good options. Perhaps if he had continued the tough policies of his predecessors, the Soviet Union could have lasted another decade. But the end, in that case, might have been extremely messy, even climaxing in another revolution.

Environmental Disaster

In addition to the political and military problems that the USSR faced, pollution was altering the geography of the nation. Since Stalin's rule, the Soviet Union had treated its natural resources as endless. The official party line was that there would always be more land to use, more water to consume, more air to breathe, and more minerals to dig out. While people in the Western world staged demonstrations in favor of stronger environmental protections, no such voices were heard in the USSR during that era.

The Soviets were now discovering that their supply of resources wasn't so endless, after all. Some of the energy sources west of the Ural Mountains had started to run low in the 1970s and 1980s. There were more resources within the USSR's borders, but many were in Siberia, one of the coldest and most remote areas on earth. Getting at them would be difficult and expensive. What's more, Soviet resource management policies weren't simply depleting the country's resources—they were damaging its environment. For example, some of the nation's good soil was eroding away because of poor land-management policies.

The state of the environment had crucial effects on the Soviet government. It couldn't easily admit that it needed to address these issues, since it was the very agency that had adopted the offending policies in the first place. Meanwhile, cleaning up after damaging environmental disasters was not going to be easy or cheap. The Soviet economy was struggling in the 1980s, and the nation could not afford the added financial burden of environmental rehabilitation.

If the Soviet leadership didn't feel a sense of urgency about the environment in 1985, it certainly did a year later when a nuclear disaster took place at a plant in Chernobyl, Ukraine. A breakdown in a reactor, combined with operator error, resulted in the release of

The Chernobyl nuclear power plant is pictured in May 1986, a few weeks after a reactor breakdown resulted in dozens of deaths.

high levels of radiation into the atmosphere. One of the causes of the accident was a poorly designed reactor.

Thousands of people had to be evacuated from the region, and the city was practically abandoned. It is unknown how many deaths the incident caused directly and indirectly. Two workers on the site died the night of the accident, and twenty-eight more died because of acute radiation poisoning in the weeks afterward. Others died due to radiation exposure later in life. The incident damaged the government's already shaky reputation.

The Soviet Union's mounting economic woes helped compel Gorbachev to take a step that would have been almost unimaginable a few years before: a major military treaty with the United States. He thought he had no choice, telling members of the Politburo, "[W]e will be pulled into an arms race that is beyond our capabilities, and we will lose it because we are at the limit of our capabilities ... If the new round [in the arms race] begins, the pressures on our economy will be unbelievable." After signing the agreement, he met with Reagan in Iceland in the fall of 1986 and discussed a second treaty that would call for a reduction in both sides' nuclear arsenals. However, they ultimately could not agree on the conditions of such a pact.

The Seeds of Change

In 1987, Gorbachev implemented two new policies that would change the way the Soviet government operated. He used two words to describe those policies: *perestroika* and *glasnost*—Russian words that would become known throughout the world.

Perestroika translates as "restructuring," and in this case, it referred to the decision to open elections on the lower levels of government to all. That meant more choices for voters, although the winners still had to follow orders from the higher echelons of the Soviet government. Economically, perestroika led to the end of price controls and the establishment of freer markets. It wasn't exactly capitalism, in which government would have tried to stay out of the way of economic forces. But it certainly was a step in that direction, as Gorbachev hoped market incentives would give a boost to the welfare of his countrymen.

The English equivalent of *glasnost* is "openness." The idea was to give the Soviet people more freedom of expression. Steps toward that goal included less media censorship. Citizens could now criticize even government officials in public, which must have been shocking after almost seventy years of strict controls.

The moves might have seemed necessary under the circumstances, but they didn't help. They may have even sped up the decline of the Soviet Union. The economic transformation needed time to take hold, but time was not on Gorbachev's side. The West had started to squeeze the Soviet economy, mostly through a worldwide decline in the price of oil—an important source of revenue for the USSR.

The Soviets had never placed much importance on the manufacturing of consumer goods, and as the economy continued to sputter, worker strikes and long lines for goods began to pop up. Clothing and shoes became scarce. Reports of crime and government corruption started to appear in the media for the first time in Soviet history.

Freedom of speech also allowed critics of the Soviet regime to become more organized. Those critics saw that the Soviet leadership was living extremely well while the people were struggling, and that added to the unrest. As they became more vocal about these inequalities, loyalty to the nation diminished.

The year 1988 saw the first tangible sign that the Soviet empire was starting to shrink. After more than eight years, the USSR began to remove its troops from Afghanistan. The costs of the invasion had been enormous. Not only had the USSR invested billions of dollars, it is estimated that sixteen thousand Soviet troops had died during the invasion and subsequent occupation. The pullout was complete by February 1989. A civil war then broke out in Afghanistan, and by 1994 a group of Muslim fundamentalists known as the Taliban had been formed. The Taliban took control of the country from 1996 to 2002.

Further cracks in the Soviet empire started to appear. Communist Party leaders in Armenia and Azerbaijan were fired after tensions heated up in the two Soviet republics. The USSR removed Janos Kadar, the Communist Party chief in Hungary. And finally, government officials released the national budget for the coming year and announced that a $58 billion deficit (more than $120 billion in today's dollars) was due to what they called "past mistakes." The Supreme Soviet—the country's legislature—was disbanded in favor of a revised political structure called the Congress of People's Deputies. Gorbachev was named leader of the new body.

By 1989, the stage was set for one of the most significant years in recent history. Almost every day seemed to feature a new, shocking event, starting on February 6 in Poland, where the seeds for change had already been sown. Negotiations began between the Polish government and Solidarity. Within two months, a deal had been reached to stage free elections and allow Solidarity to become a legal political party.

N o one could have foreseen the remarkable life of Lech Walesa—not even Walesa himself. He began his career as a labor worker in Poland but went on to become a Nobel Prize winner and the president of his newly independent country.

Walesa was born in 1943 in Popowo, Poland. He became a car mechanic in the early 1960s, and then spent two years in the army before landing an electrician's job in the Gdansk shipyards.

In 1970, Walesa was involved in a Gdansk workers' strike over rising food prices. Thirty workers died in the unrest. Six years later, he was fired from his position as a shop steward because of his ongoing participation in strikes and illegal unions. Walesa worked some temporary jobs while staying in touch with the shipyard workers and continuing to organize trade unions in Gdansk, where he was kept under surveillance by the government.

In 1980, Walesa and his fellow ship workers took the then-unprecedented step of going on strike. Solidarity, as the union was called, demanded more rights for workers, and it

Lech Walesa became an unexpected agent for change in Poland.

won some important victories: the right to organize and form an independent union.

The early years of the 1980s were bright and hopeful for Walesa and the union. Walesa traveled around the world and even met with Pope John Paul II at the Vatican. However, new challenges emerged. The Polish leadership cracked down on the union's newly won freedoms, in part because it feared a Soviet military invasion resembling those that had taken place in other Eastern European nations. Walesa was interned in a rural house for eleven months then went back to work in Gdansk in 1982; his union still was not permitted to act according to its previously earned rights. Walesa won the Nobel Peace Prize in 1983, a commendation that was attacked by the Polish government.

As the economy spiraled downward in 1980s, General Wojciech Jaruzelski, leader of the Polish government, was forced to negotiate with the workers. The talks came with the knowledge that Mikhail Gorbachev of the Soviet Union was no longer willing to send in troops to enforce control of the nation.

Then, in 1989 came a shocking development—Poland and other Eastern European nations were freed from Soviet control. About a year later, Walesa was elected president of the republic of Poland. It was the first free election for the nation's presidency in sixty-three years. Walesa worked to transition the nation's economy to a free-market system. He was president until November 1995, when he lost a reelection bid.

Walesa will be remembered forever as a crucial figure in the history of Poland and in the dissolution of the USSR.

On March 26, free elections were held for positions in the Congress of People's Deputies. The Soviet people sent a strong message, handing the Communist Party a string of embarrassing defeats. Boris Yeltsin, the future leader of the Russian Federation, was elected as a congressional delegate.

In June, about two hundred fifty thousand Hungarians met to mark the reburial of one of the leaders of their 1956 revolution attempt, which was crushed by Soviet troops. Travel restrictions between east and west were eliminated, and many scrambled across the border to Austria and away from Communist control. October saw free elections in Hungary.

However, the most dramatic moment of the year came in Berlin, where the wall between the eastern and western halves of the city was the most visible symbol of the Cold War. Its construction in 1961 had exacerbated already-tense United States–USSR relations. On November 9, all East German borders were opened, and thousands swarmed around the wall. Some danced on top of it, while others chopped away at it. The two Germanys, East and West, formally reunified soon after. Most of the other Eastern European nations fell out of the Soviet sphere of influence within a few months. The USSR's empire had suffered a severe blow from which it would never recover.

The final steps toward the collapse of the Soviet Union came in August of 1991, when hard-line members of the Communist Party gathered to try to overthrow the government. Gorbachev was placed under house arrest, and it was announced over state radio that an emergency committee had taken control of the government. The plotters, however, made several wrong moves. There were no arrests, allowing Yeltsin— now the newly elected president of the country and a vocal critic of the Communist elite—to lead a counter-revolt. Military forces refused to follow the emergency committee's orders, and Yeltsin's speech to the masses in Moscow from atop a tank became an iconic moment. Soon, the leaders of the coup were either dead by suicide or in jail.

Ironically, the plotters sped up the journey toward the Soviet Union's final collapse. By the end of 1991, most of the constituent republics were ready to break apart; the exceptions were in central Asia, where the nations had weaker economies. On Christmas Day, Gorbachev resigned as leader of the USSR, but not before signing the Belavezha Accords, which officially dissolved the Soviet Union.

Later that day, the Soviet flag came down the flagpole in the Kremlin, a stronghold of the Soviet government. It was replaced by the Russian flag for the first time in more than six decades.

The effects of 1989 continued to rumble into 1990. Eastern European nations were taking formal steps to break away from Soviet control. Gorbachev was awarded the Nobel Peace Prize in 1990 for his role in allowing the Eastern European states to control their own destiny.

Meanwhile, a desire for democracy had spread across the border and into the Soviet Union. Military power was called up to suppress protests in some of the central Asian republics, while

The Soviet Union is pictured in 1989, just before its collapse brought about the independence of many Soviet Republics, such as Kazakhstan (*in orange*), Ukraine (*in yellow, top left*), and Belarus (*in green, top left*).

other parts of the USSR took more drastic steps. Lithuania declared its independence on March 11, 1990, the first republic to do so. The small nation on the Baltic Sea was invaded by Russian troops less than a year later but eventually became independent.

By the time the Russian Federation was formed, the borders of the once-powerful Soviet Union had been entirely redrawn. Russia was flanked by a host of newly independent nations that had once been a symbol of Soviet strength.

Today's Russian Federation (*shown in peach*) is much smaller than the USSR once was, surrounded as it is with former Soviet Republics. It remains a powerful and influential nation on the world stage.

CHAPTER FIVE

The Rebirth of Russia

By early 1992, the former Soviet Union's borders had been dramatically redrawn, and world maps needed a major revision after so much turbulence had taken place. Russian borders were more or less back to where they had been before the Soviet Union was founded in 1922.

Russia was, in many ways, a much weaker nation than its immediate predecessor had been. Former Soviet republics were planning for the future, while Eastern European nations that had been under Soviet control for forty years were also preparing for major changes. Some of these countries looked to the West for political and economic support, while others remained closely tied to Russia.

In the meantime, Russia's economy still faced huge problems. With the collapse of Communism, Russia

Opposite: A giant statue of Vladimir Lenin in Germany was taken down and buried in 1991.

Boris Yeltsin, the first president of Russia, faced many problems after the fall of the Soviet Union.

had taken its first tentative steps toward capitalism, a transition that some called "shock therapy" because there were sure to be painful challenges ahead before citizens saw an improvement in their quality of life. Price controls were dropped, and inflation ran rampant, to as much as 2,400 percent in 1992. The gross domestic product—a leading measure of economic activity and standard of living—shrank by 30 percent.

Social Challenges

Also alarming was the fact that the population of Russia was shrinking, even though more people were moving to Russia than were leaving. There were 148 million people in Russia in 1992 and 144 million in 2016. How could the population go down? With

FUTURE POPULATION CHALLENGES

Experts believe Russia's population could drop to 111 million by 2050. This could cause economic challenges, such as a decrease in housing construction and a reduced need for recreation, cultural facilities, and mass transit.

the global population growing exponentially, most countries' populations grow as well. However, as is common during difficult economic times, Russian couples were having fewer babies than were needed to keep the overall numbers stable. Abortions, which had peaked in 1988 at 4.6 million, were still at 3.44 million in 1992. That's compared to the actual number of births—1.56 million. What's more, the mortality rate had increased. Life expectancy for men dropped by six years between 1990 and 1994 to about fifty-eight years, compared to the global average of about sixty-four years for men in 1994. Russian women fared better: their life expectancy was seventy-two years, compared to the global average of sixty-eight—but their life expectancy had also declined since 1990, from seventy-four years.

The Communist government had set up something of a safety net for all its citizens: everyone had worked somewhere, and companies were usually responsible for taking care of their workers. However, when businesses were privatized early on in Russia's rebirth, the safety net disappeared for many. For example, companies that manufactured weapons laid off workers in a post–Cold War world.

These and other challenges made the transition from a Soviet state to a federation a miserable experience for many Russian citizens. The country's power and prestige hit record lows, and people needed a scapegoat. The prime target became Mikhail Gorbachev, who had signed the declaration breaking up the Soviet Union. He experienced the outrage of his fellow citizens whenever he walked out the door. However, Gorbachev had a ready answer to those who screamed at him: "Remember, I am the one who gave you the right to shout."

In addition to more freedom of speech, Russians now had expanded religious freedoms. Lenin had famously described religion as "the opium of the people." He wanted to lead a nation of atheists, and those with religious beliefs were not allowed to be members of the Communist Party. With these restrictions finally lifted, many outsiders expected a huge resurgence in the popularity of organized religion, particularly among adherents of the Russian Orthodox Church, which had been the dominant faith in the country for centuries.

However, there was no major boost in church attendance after 1991. And in fact, new religious restrictions were put in place: a law was passed in Russia in 1997 to make it difficult for religions other than Russian Orthodox Christianity to thrive. Still, there

Opposite: The Church of the Savior on Spilled Blood in St. Petersburg is one of the best-known edifices associated with the Russian Orthodox Church.

are some exceptions within Russia, depending on the history and geography of specific regions. Students at Armenian schools must take a course on the history of the Armenian Apostolic Church, and Islam is practiced in regions along Russia's southern border.

Russia's First President

The new leader of Russia, Boris Yeltsin, could be called the first true president in the nation's history. Before the revolution of 1917, royal families had led the Russian Empire for centuries. When the Bolsheviks took control, Vladimir Lenin became the leader of Russia; neither he nor any of his successors were elected by popular vote.

Yeltsin was an engineer who joined the Communist Party in 1961 at the age of thirty. In 1985, Gorbachev's team recruited him to serve as head of the construction department, and he was soon effectively the mayor of Moscow. Along the way, he became known for his eagerness to spend time with average citizens, even taking public transportation to work.

Yeltsin later disagreed with Gorbachev over the pace of reform, and the two grew apart. In 1991, Yeltsin won the first-ever open election for president of Russia.

Yeltsin's initial years as president were not easy. One of his biggest challenges came in September 1993, when—in response to increasing political resistance to his free-market reforms—he decided to dissolve Russia's parliament, an unconstitutional act. That

A pro-Communist crowd numbering in the thousands gathers in Moscow on September 24, 1993, to protest President Boris Yeltsin's decree dissolving the Russian parliament.

led to a massive, nonviolent sit-in. Tensions escalated in October, however, as protesters and government authorities clashed in an attempted coup. Hundreds of people died, and several Moscow landmarks were damaged. Many felt that Yeltsin had lost touch with average Russians, having instead developed a taste for the expensive benefits of high office and trading in public transportation for limousines. Yeltsin had transformed from a popular figure in the public eye to an overreaching leader akin to a dictator.

Despite an unsuccessful military campaign against Chechen rebels and lagging economic growth, Yeltsin was reelected in 1996. He faced continued clashes with fellow government officials—even firing his entire cabinet in 1998—before he resigned on December 31, 1999, naming Vladimir Putin the acting president of Russia.

Unrest in Chechnya

Tensions grew in some areas of the former Soviet Union in the early 1990s. Chechnya is a small, landlocked republic in southwestern Russia, located west of the Caspian Sea. People of the region had never been treated well by the Soviets. In 1944, Joseph Stalin had deported about half a million Chechens to Siberia for allegedly collaborating with Nazi Germany, though the real motive for the mass deportation may have been that Chechens had always proven difficult to suppress, even mounting a revolt against collectivization in 1929. Half of them died on the way to Siberia. Others perished in brutal conditions; many were even thrown into the snow and told they were on their own. Those who survived were not allowed to return to Chechnya until 1957. These events had fomented a level of mistrust between the Chechens and the Russians that survives to this day.

Chechnya had planned to become an independent nation in the
1990s, but Russia had other ideas, invading Chechnya in 1994.

When the Soviet Union started to break apart in the early 1990s, Chechnya ousted its Soviet-backed president, and after a coup led by politician and former general Dzhokhar Dudayev, elected Dudayev president; he declared Chechnya's independence from Russia the next month. However, the new Russian government did not want Chechnya to become a separate nation, for fear that other Russian republics might follow its example. Yeltsin ignored Chechnya's complaints for more than two years until, in 1994, Russia invaded Chechnya, sparking a two-year war that would kill as many as a hundred thousand people, including Dudayev. The small republic was almost wiped off the map, and in the end, it was forced to remain a part of the Russian Federation.

The year 1999 saw three apartment building bombings in three Russian cities; 243 people were killed and 1,742 wounded. Prime Minister Vladimir Putin blamed the bombings on Chechen secessionists, though this has never been conclusively proven. Putin nevertheless earned praise and popularity for taking a tough stand against the terrorists. Russian forces entered Chechnya again, and after years of violence, installed a Russian-backed president in 2007; Chechnya has been led by pro-Russian political leaders ever since.

However, problems between the two sides persist. Chechnya still has an active resistance group. Some say that Russia has refused the small republic independence because oil drilling and refining were once major industries there and contributed greatly to the overall

Vladimir Putin of Russia, pictured here in 2001, ranks as one of the most powerful leaders in the world.

Russian economy. Others argue that the suppression is the result of a cultural and religious divide between Russians and Chechens, a high percentage of whom are Muslim.

Growing Stability, Ongoing Border Disputes

Conditions have improved in Russia since its rocky rebirth, and its vast geography has helped smooth the transition. The nation still has large supplies of oil and natural gas, which make for profitable exports, and Russia's economy finally showed some sustained growth starting around 2000—also the year that Vladimir Putin began his tenure as the leader of Russia.

Putin was born in St. Petersburg—then called Leningrad—in 1952. He worked for the KGB, the Soviet Union's agency for foreign intelligence and domestic security, until 1990. After retiring from that organization, Putin became a politician, first serving as deputy mayor of St. Petersburg.

In 1998, Yeltsin recruited Putin to serve as the government's link to regional governments throughout Russia. From there, he was named head of the Federal Security Service, which served some of the same functions as the now-defunct KGB. After Yeltsin fired his prime minister, Sergey Stepashin, in 1999, he picked Putin as a replacement on an interim basis. Putin was elected president in 2000 and reelected in

2004. He couldn't serve another consecutive term in 2008 but was picked as the prime minister by the new president, Dmitry Medvedev. In 2012, Putin won a third term as president and picked Medvedev as his prime minister.

It's difficult to say how much credit Putin deserves for Russia's economic growth during the twenty-first century, but it can't be denied that times have improved. Some key freedoms—including gay rights and the freedom of expression—have suffered under Putin's tutelage. The economy, however—while still not completely embracing capitalism—grew after the sluggish 1990s and shows few signs of returning to the complete government control that characterized the Soviet era.

Still, Putin and the Russian leadership appear to have remained on edge about the activities of some of the country's neighbors. Georgia was one such neighbor. It's a relatively small country between Russia and Turkey and has a coastline on the Black Sea. It declared its independence in April 1991. Almost immediately, South Ossetia—a piece of territory located on the Russian border—declared its independence from Georgia, and Abkhazia—in western Georgia—followed South Ossetia's lead. The Russians offered support to separatist groups, hoping to maintain some influence in that region. Military action broke out between Georgia and the rebel states until Russia brokered a cease-fire in 1994 and sent peacekeeping troops into the region.

CONFLICT WITH UKRAINE

Ukraine has long had powerful neighbors, and as a result, the small country has often found itself in harm's way during regional military conflicts. Such problems temporarily abated when Ukraine was part of the USSR, but when it declared its independence in 1991, the potential for such conflicts was renewed.

The Russians took notice when Ukraine started the process of joining NATO in 2002; after all, the North Atlantic Treaty Organization had been a united front against Communism after World War II. A little more than two years later, pro-Russian politician Viktor Yanukovych was elected president of Ukraine in an election that was immediately described as rigged by opposing parties. The Ukrainian supreme court ordered a new election, and this time Viktor Yushchenko won the election. Yanukovych rebounded by winning the 2010 presidential election, and Ukraine's parliament later voted to withdraw its application to join NATO.

In 2013, thousands protested the government's decision not to join the European Union. Yanukovych left the country for Russia in 2014, and an opposing political party took over. That was all the provocation that Russian leader Vladimir Putin needed to take a dramatic step that would alter the geography of the region.

Russian troops moved into Crimea, a Ukrainian territory and peninsula protruding into the Black Sea, claiming that ethnic Russians in Ukraine needed to be liberated. The offensive angered the rest of the world and resulted in casualties on both sides.

Analysts could only guess at the motives behind Russia's invasion. Some believe Russia wanted to regain some of the territory it had lost in the breakup of the Soviet Union. Crimea had been part of Russia from 1783 to 1954, when it was transferred to Ukraine. Others noted the peninsula's strategic importance, guarding the entry into the Sea of Azov from the Black Sea or its access to untapped natural resources such as oil deposits in the

Black Sea, pointing out that the invasion helped Russia's chances of controlling a larger share of that market.

Some analysts also believe the invasion was an attempt to keep Western influences from moving too close to Russia's borders. If so, the plan may have been unsuccessful. In 2017, Ukrainian president Petro Poroshenko pledged to work on reforms that would qualify the country for NATO membership by 2020.

No matter the reasoning, the Russian invasion was only the latest in a series of aggressive actions that have taken place on Ukrainian soil for centuries.

Ukraine is shown in dark brown above. A dispute over the Crimean Peninsula, which juts into the Black Sea, led to an attack by Russian forces in 2014. The Crimea was annexed by Russia, though mapmakers still don't agree as to whether the peninsula belongs to Russia or Ukraine.

The relationship between Georgia and Russia had been strained for a long time. After the conflict, Georgia's foreign policy team was still inexperienced, and Russia was anxious to influence events there. On August 7, 2008, hostilities broke out again. South Ossete rebels attacked Georgian peacekeeping forces; Georgia responded by sending troops into the region, and Russia flew airplanes over Georgian territory, shooting missiles into South Ossetia. Three days later, Russian tanks and military personnel drove through South Ossetia and into Georgian territory. On August 12, the Russians agreed to a peace plan, and another cease-fire was signed on August 15.

The status of those separatist territories was still in flux at the end of 2017. South Ossetia was recognized as independent by Russia, Nicaragua, Venezuela, and Nauru, a small island in the Pacific Ocean. However, Georgia and the rest of the world have not recognized the region as a separate political entity. It's the same story in Abkhazia, which is supported by Russia and few others. The potential for conflict among neighbors remains high.

The map of Russia and its neighbors changed again in 2014, when Russia annexed Crimea, part of the Ukraine. It was a risky maneuver for Putin and his government, but it met with the approval of the Russian people.

Putin's aggressive approach to maintaining or even expanding Russia's borders has strengthened the country's image as a powerful global force. Relations with the United States, however, have frequently been rocky during his time in office. It remains to be seen how the Russians' alleged tampering with the 2016 American presidential election will affect US-Russian relations. Meanwhile, Putin has worked to improve Russia's relationship with such Asian nations as China, whose leadership has stated that the two countries have never been closer.

Putin also took other steps to improve his nation's standing on the world stage. Russia won the right to stage the 2014 Winter Olympics in Sochi, a city on the Black Sea. It also won the bid to host the 2018 World Cup, the world's top soccer event. Russia did take a hit to its reputation, though, when the Olympic International Committee banned the nation from competing in the 2018 Winter Olympics amid allegations of a state-run doping program. Many Russian athletes were still allowed to compete as independents.

No matter who leads Russia in the decades to come, the nation's geography will play a role in the country's fate. Russia's immense size and ample natural resources guarantee that it will remain a prominent and influential voice in world events.

CHRONOLOGY

•882 CE   The Kievan Rus—the first government formed by what came to be known as the Russian people—is formed in eastern Europe. It is organized by Prince Oleg, who places the capital in Kiev.

•1236   The Mongols rampage through Europe, defeating the Kievan Rus and ending its 354-year history as a nation.

•1283   The city-state of Muscovy is formed in the area around present-day Moscow.

•1462   Ivan the Great becomes the leader of Muscovy and triples the kingdom's size. Territory from Finland to the Ural Mountains comes under Muscovy's control.

•1547   Ivan the Terrible takes over as tsar of Muscovy, and his armies gain control of more land, stretching from Moscow to the Ural Mountains in the east and to the Caspian Sea to the south.

•1580   Russia begins an eighty-year campaign to claim most of Siberia as its own; it meets with little opposition.

•1638   Russian explorers reach the Pacific Ocean, where they continue to claim territory for Muscovy.

•1712   The city of St. Petersburg is founded on the Baltic Sea, and Russian leader Peter the Great moves the nation's capital there from Moscow.

•1741   Russians first land in what is now called Alaska and will establish colonies there in the years afterward.

•1762   Russia begins to annex new territory, including part of Poland and some land around the Black Sea, during the thirty-four-year reign of Catherine the Great.

•1812   French emperor Napoleon I sends five hundred thousand soldiers into Russia. After initial successes, French soldiers are forced to retreat, leaving Russian borders unchanged.

•1867   Russia sells Alaska to the United States for $7.2 million ($113.8 million in today's dollars).

•1917   The Russian Revolution overthrows Tsar Nicholas II; he is replaced by Vladimir Lenin.

•1922   Russia, Belarus, Ukraine, Azerbaijan, Armenia, and Georgia join together to form the Union of Soviet Socialist Republics, or USSR.

•1945   World War II ends, marking the beginning of the Soviet Union's political control over the nations of Eastern Europe during a post-war occupation of the region.

•1979   Soviet forces invade Afghanistan.

•**1980**   Dock workers in the Polish city of Gdansk go on strike. The uprising leads to an agreement with the Polish government giving unions the right to exist and strike.

•**1981**   An assassination attempt is made on Pope John Paul II. Evidence suggests that the Soviet Union may have ordered the attack in an attempt to maintain control of Eastern European countries.

•**1985**   Mikhail Gorbachev is selected as the new leader of the Soviet Union.

•**1986**   A nuclear meltdown takes place at a reactor in Chernobyl, Ukraine, spreading radiation as far as France and killing at least thirty people immediately.

•**1988**   Soviet troops begin to pull out of Afghanistan after eight years.

•**1989**   The nations of Eastern Europe become independent from Soviet control. The Berlin Wall falls.

•**1991**   The various republics of the Soviet Union break away. The dissolution of the USSR is formally signed into law by Gorbachev on December 25.

•**2008**   Russia and Georgia engage in a brief military skirmish.

•**2014**   Russian troops take control of Crimea, a peninsula in the Black Sea that was previously part of the Ukraine.

Age of Imperialism An era during which several European nations sought to control territory in other parts of the world. It is considered to have started in 1763, when Great Britain took control of India, and to have ended with the outbreak of World War I.

Alexander the Great An emperor who reigned from 356 to 323 BCE. His empire included territory from Greece and Egypt to India.

arable Suitable for growing crops.

Bolshevik A member of the Russian Social Democratic Party, which became known as the Communist Party after its victory in the Russian Revolution in October 1917.

Cold War The nonviolent conflict between the United States and Soviet Union from 1945 to 1991.

collaboration A situation in which two people or groups work together toward a common goal.

collectivization The grouping of farms owned by peasants into a single, much larger unit. Russian leader Joseph Stalin implemented a collectivization policy in the late 1920s and early 1930s in an effort to increase food production.

containment An attempt to keep something harmful under control and within some limits. Here, it refers to the policy of the United States and its allies to stop the spread of Communism after World War II.

doctrine A set of beliefs usually associated with religion or politics.

GLOSSARY

European Union A group of nations that banded together in attempt to form common policies, mostly with regards to economic matters.

faction A group that splits off from a larger group to support its own particular cause or belief.

Great Purge A time of repression and persecution in the Soviet Union. Between 1936 and 1938, more than 1.5 million people were arrested and almost seven hundred thousand were killed.

gross domestic product The total of all goods and services produced by a nation in a specific time period (usually a year). It is the leading tool for measuring economic activity and standard of living.

hard-line Unwilling to compromise; strict. This was a word often used to describe US and Soviet attitudes during the Cold War.

hegemony Influence or authority over others; the social, ideological, cultural, or economic influence exerted by a dominant country or group.

intern To hold captive.

KGB The Komitet Gosudarstvennoy Bezopasnosti, which served as the main security agency for the Soviet Union from 1954 to 1991. The KGB worked in such areas as espionage and intelligence gathering.

kulak A peasant in the pre-Soviet Russia and the Soviet Union who was wealthy enough to own land and hire workers.

mortality rate The number of deaths in a particular period of time.

Ottoman Empire A territory controlled by Turkish tribes that extended into Europe, Asia, and Africa. Its six-hundred-year reign ended in 1922, at the end of World War I.

puppet government A government that has outward signs of self-rule or legitimacy but in reality is controlled by outside forces.

Roman Empire Lands controlled by the capital city of Rome from 27 BCE to 476 CE. At its peak, it controlled territory in much of Europe, as well as parts of Asia and North Africa.

satellite nations A term used to refer to countries under the control of another nation. It was first used to describe the nations of Eastern Europe that, after World War II, were controlled by the Soviet Union.

scapegoat Someone who is blamed for the mistakes of others.

separatist A person who seeks to separate a particular group from another group. The word is often used in association with political or religious groups.

sit-in A protest in which a group occupies a particular piece of territory and refuses to leave until its demands are met.

sphere of influence An area of the world in which one nation dominates the political landscape and has a great influence over other nations' actions.

status quo Latin for "existing state."

Supreme Soviet The top governing group within the Soviet Union.

tsar An emperor of Russia before 1917. It is derived from the Latin word *caesar*, which had come to refer to any leader of the Roman Empire.

FURTHER INFORMATION

Books

Bartlett, Roger. *A History of Russia*. New York: Macmillan, 2005.

Blinnikov, Mikhail S. *A Geography of Russia and Its Neighbors*. New York: The Guilford Press, 2011.

Chakravarti, C. N., and A. K. Basu. *Soviet Union: Land and People*. New Delhi, India: Northern Book Centre, 1987.

Kort, Michael G. *The Handbook of the Former Soviet Union*. Brookfield, CT: Millbrook Press, 1997.

————. *The Soviet Colossus: A History of the USSR*. New York: Charles Scribner's Sons, 1985.

Websites

Reporting the Russian Revolution
www.bl.uk/russian-revolution/articles/reporting-the-russian-revolution

The British Library explains how Russia's revolution and civil wars were represented in the media at the time and explains how the press was used to persuade and even manipulate the public.

Russia and the Curse of Geography
www.theatlantic.com/international/archive/2015/10/russia-geography-ukraine-syria/413248

This in-depth article explains how geography influences Russian president Vladimir Putin's decision-making.

Soviet Union Timeline
www.bbc.com/news/world-europe-17858981

From the Russian Revolution to Gorbachev's resignation, learn key events in the history of the USSR.

Videos

History of Russia
www.youtube.com/watch?v=mnS9kr64bPM

Starting with the Kievan Rus, view changes in Russian geography over the course of history.

Russia: Climate, Vegetation, Wildlife, Resources, Industry, Transport, Trade, and People
www.youtube.com/watch?v=0kLAN6-PJJI.

Learn key facts that will help you understand what it's like to live in Russia, from weather to culture.

Russia's Geography Problem
www.youtube.com/watch?v=v3C_5bsdQWg

Dive into the geographical challenges that affect the Russian economy and the quality of life in the country.

BIBLIOGRAPHY

Applebaum, Anne. "How the Pope 'Defeated Communism.'" *Washington Post*, April 6, 2005. http://www. washingtonpost.com/wp-dyn/articles/A28398-2005Apr5. html.

Arab Gateway to Ukraine. "Agriculture." 2007–2014. http:// www.ukraine-arabia.ae/economy/agriculture.

Atomic Archive. "Cold War: A Brief History—Reagan's Star Wars." Accessed October 3, 2017. http://www. atomicarchive.com/History/coldwar/page20.shtml.

Bartlett, Roger. *A History of Russia*. New York: Macmillan, 2005.

BBC. "Ukraine Profile—Timeline." August 2, 2017. http:// www.bbc.co.uk/news/world-europe-18010123.

Biography. "Catherine II." October 31, 2017. https://www. biography.com/people/catherine-ii-9241622.

———. "Mikhail Sergeyevich Gorbachev." January 22, 2016. https://www.biography.com/people/mikhail-sergeyevich-gorbachev-9315721.

Borgisky, Bjorn. "Russian Economic Geography." Economy Watch, August 6, 2009. http://www.economywatch.com/ economy-business-and-finance-news/Russia_Economic_ Geography_08-09.html.

Catholic Straight Answers. "What Was John Paul II's Role in the Fall of the Soviet Union?" Accessed September 27, 2017. http://catholicstraightanswers.com/pope-john-paul-iis-role-fall-soviet-union.

Chakravarti, C. N., and A. K. Basu. *Soviet Union: Land and People*. New Delhi, India: Northern Book Centre, 1987.

CNN. "2008 Russia Georgia Conflict Fast Facts." March 26, 2017. http://www.cnn.com/2014/03/13/world/ europe/2008-georgia-russia-conflict/index.html.

BIBLIOGRAPHY

Encyclopædia Britannica. "Continental System." February 16, 2016. https://www.britannica.com/event/Continental-System.

———. "Kievan Rus." February 22, 2016. https://www.britannica.com/topic/Kievan-Rus.

———. "Russo-Japanese War." March 15, 2017. https://www.britannica.com/event/Russo-Japanese-War.

Encyclopedia of World Biography. "Boris Yeltsin Biography." 2017. http://www.notablebiographies.com/We-Z/Yeltsin-Boris.html.

Frazier, Ian. "Travels in Siberia—I: The Ultimate Road Trip." *New Yorker*, August 3, 2009. https://www.newyorker.com/magazine/2009/08/03/travels-in-siberia-i.

Gascoigne, Bamber. "History of Afghanistan." HistoryWorld. Accessed October 18, 2018. http://www.historyworld.net/about/sources.asp?gtrack=pthc.

Geographic.org. "Soviet Union Geography—1991." 2003. https://theodora.com/wfb1991/soviet_union/soviet_union_geography.html.

Gitomirski, Sasha. "Glasnost and Perestroika." The Cold War Museum. Accessed October 4, 2017. http://www.coldwar.org/articles/80s/glasnostandperestroika.asp.

Greenspan, Jesse. "Why Napoleon's Invasion of Russia Was the Beginning of the End." History Channel, June 22, 2012. http://www.history.com/news/napoleons-disastrous-invasion-of-russia-200-years-ago.

Hays, Jeffrey. "Creation of the Soviet Union and Early Soviet Foreign Policy." Facts and Details, May 2016. http://factsanddetails.com/russia/History/sub9_1d/entry-4961.html.

History Channel. "Cold War: 1984—Chernenko Becomes General Secretary." 2017. http://www.history.com/this-day-in-history/chernenko-becomes-general-secretary.

Iggiagruk Hensley, William L. "Why Russia Gave Up Alaska, America's Gateway to the Arctic." Conversation, March 29, 2017. http://theconversation.com/why-russia-gave-up-alaska-americas-gateway-to-the-arctic-74675.

Investopedia. "European Union—EU." 2017. https://www.investopedia.com/terms/e/europeanunion.asp.

Kort, Michael G. *The Handbook of the Former Soviet Union*. Brookfield, CT: Millbrook Press, 1997.

———. *The Soviet Colossus: A History of the USSR*. New York: Charles Scribner's Sons, 1985.

Kramer, Mark. "The Rise and Fall of Solidarity." *New York Times*, December 12, 2011. http://www.nytimes.com/2011/12/13/opinion/the-rise-and-fall-of-solidarity.html?mcubz=0.

Kucha, Glenn, and Jennifer Llewellyn. "Sino-Soviet Relations." Alpha History, 2015. Accessed November 21, 2017. http://alphahistory.com/chineserevolution/sino-soviet-relations.

Live Science. "Ancient City Ruled by Genghis Khan's Heirs Is Unearthed in Russia." NBC News, October 24, 2014. https://www.nbcnews.com/science/science-news/ancient-city-ruled-genghis-khans-heirs-unearthed-russia-n233491.

Luhn, Alec. "15 Years of Vladimir Putin: 15 Ways He Has Changed Russia and the World." *Guardian*, May 6, 2015. https://www.theguardian.com/world/2015/may/06/vladimir-putin-15-ways-he-changed-russia-world.

Manaev, Georgy. "Why Did Russia Sell Alaska to the United States?" Russia Beyond, April 21, 2014. https://www.rbth.com/arts/2014/04/20/why_did_russia_sell_alaska_to_the_united_states_36061.html.

Maranzani, Barbara. "8 Things You Didn't Know About Catherine the Great." History Channel, July 9, 2012.

http://www.history.com/news/8-things-you-didnt-know-about-catherine-the-great.

Marshall, Tim. "Russia and the Curse of Geography." *Atlantic*, October 31, 2015. https://www.theatlantic.com/international/archive/2015/10/russia-geography-ukraine-syria/413248.

Myers, Steven Lee. "Russia Closes File on Three 1999 Bombings." *New York Times*, May 1, 2003. http://www.nytimes.com/2003/05/01/world/russia-closes-file-on-three-1999-bombings.html.

The Nobel Foundation. "Lech Walesa—Biographical." Nobelprize.org, 1983. http://www.nobelprize.org/nobel_prizes/peace/laureates/1983/walesa-bio.html.

Norwich University. "Exploring 5 Reasons for the Collapse of the Soviet Union." July 2016. http://graduate.norwich.edu/resources-mmh/articles-mmh/exploring-5-reasons-for-the-collapse-of-the-soviet-union.

PBS. "A Historical Timeline of Afghanistan." May 4, 2011. http://www.pbs.org/newshour/updates/asia-jan-june11-timeline-afghanistan.

Pelletier, Rodney. "New Book Reveals Soviets Behind Attempted Assassination of Pope St. John Paul II." Church Militant, May 2, 2017. https://www.churchmilitant.com/news/article/new-book-reveals-soviets-behind-attempted-assassination-of-st.-john-paul-ii.

Pifer, Steven. "Will Ukraine Join NATO? A Course for Disappointment." Brookings Institution, July 25, 2017. https://www.brookings.edu/blog/order-from-chaos/2017/07/25/will-ukraine-join-nato-a-course-for-disappointment.

RussianGeography.com. "The East European Plain: Land Forms." Accessed September 25, 2017. http://

russiangeography.com/European_plain/east-european-plain-land-forms.

Russiapedia. "On This Day: Russia in a Click—8 February." 2005–2017. https://russiapedia.rt.com/on-this-day/february-8.

Sahakyan, Armine. "Hopes of Religious Freedom in Former Soviet Union Fall Short." *HuffPost*. Accessed October 26, 2017. https://www.huffingtonpost.com/armine-sahakyan/hopes-of-religious-freedo_b_9509396.html.

Sebestyen, Victor. "The K.G.B.'s Bathhouse Plot." *New York Times*, August 20, 2011. http://www.nytimes.com/2011/08/21/opinion/sunday/the-soviet-coup-that-failed.html.

Smitha, Frank E. "Time of Troubles: 1584 to Tsar Michael in 1613." Macrohistory and World Timeline, 2001–2015. http://www.fsmitha.com/h3/h20russ2.htm.

Szczepanski, Kallie. "Afghanistan: Facts and History." ThoughtCo, March 8, 2017. https://www.thoughtco.com/afghanistan-facts-and-history-195107.

United States Department of State, Office of the Historian. "Purchase of Alaska, 1867." Accessed November 21, 2017. https://history.state.gov/milestones/1866-1898/alaska-purchase.

University of Minnesota, World Regional Geography. "The USSR and the Russian Federation." Accessed October 25, 2017. http://open.lib.umn.edu/worldgeography/chapter/3-2-the-ussr-and-the-russian-federation.

The World Bank. "Life Expectancy at Birth, Female (Years)." 2017. https://data.worldbank.org/indicator/SP.DYN.LE00.FE.IN?end=2015&start=1991.

———. "Life Expectancy at Birth, Male (Years)." 2017. https://data.worldbank.org/indicator/SP.DYN.LE00.MA.IN.

INDEX

Budd Bailey recently retired as a sports editor and reporter for the *Buffalo News*. Before joining the News in 1993, he worked for the Buffalo Sabres hockey team and WEBR Radio. Bailey is currently writing and broadcasting for several outlets. He and his wife, Jody, live in Buffalo, New York. Bailey has written books on a wide range of historical topics. His book *Red Scare: Communists in America* covered the Soviet Union's attempts at influencing the United States during the Cold War.